ICE-CREAM

Favourite Foods

Cake
Chips
Chocolate
Ice-Cream
Milkshake
Pizza

All words that appear in **bold** are explained in the glossary on page 30

First published in 1992 by
Wayland (Publishers) Ltd
61 Western Road, Hove
East Sussex BN3 1JD, England
© Copyright 1992 Wayland (Publishers) Ltd

Editor: Francesca Motisi
Research: Anne Moses and Mike and Maria Gordon

British Library Cataloguing in Publication Data
Moses, Brian
　　Ice-cream.—(Favourite Foods Series)
　　I. Title　II. Gordon, Mike　III. Series
　　641.3

　　ISBN 0-7502-0517-2

Typeset by Dorchester Typesetting Group Ltd
Printed and bound in Belgium by Casterman, S.A.

ICE-CREAM

Written by Brian Moses

Illustrated by Mike Gordon

Wayland

When did you last eat ice-cream?

Was it a jumbo size cone,
or a crunchy choc-ice?

Was it an ice-cream sundae,

or a peppermint scoop?

The Chinese invented ice-cream over 3000 years ago.

They mixed the juice of oranges
and lemons with ice and snow
from the mountains.

The Italian **explorer** Marco Polo brought back the recipe for ice-cream from China over 700 years ago.

Later on in history honey and milk were added to the recipe.

Ice-cream became very popular when the first fridges were invented.

Nowadays people in the USA eat more ice-cream than anyone else, and many enjoy visiting ice-cream parlours.

In an ice-cream factory, a **computer**-driven machine can make up to 32,000 litres each hour. How long would it take you to eat that much?

The ice-cream is made by mixing milk, fat and sugar. Sometimes fruit, nuts and flavourings are added.

The mixture is then **blended** together,

pasteurised

and cooled.

15

Before being fully frozen, the mixture
is whipped to include air. Then it is
frozen completely.

Now the ice-cream is shaped, cut, and
sometimes sprayed with chocolate.
Then it is packed.

Boxes of ice-cream and lollies are kept in giant freezers. The **temperature** in the freezers is kept at −27°C.

Penguins may like that temperature, but people who work in the freezers can't stay inside them for very long!

Fifty or sixty years ago when your grandparents were children, they probably bought their ice-creams from *STOP ME AND BUY ONE* trikes.

Today our ice-cream is delivered to shops and supermarkets in trucks with big freezers.

This group of children are about to make Peach **Sundae.** If you make this at home you will need help with opening the tin and cutting the fruit.

For the sauce you will need:

175g (6oz) raspberries (fresh or frozen)
1–2 tablespoons of sieved icing sugar
Large tin of sliced peaches in
fruit juice
Sliced kiwi-fruit
2 good scoops or spoons of vanilla
ice-cream per person
Fan-shaped ice-cream wafers (or others)
4 glass dishes

This is what you do:

1 Defrost raspberries if frozen. (They will need a few hours). If fresh, wash the raspberries and then press through a sieve with a wooden spoon. Mix in the icing sugar.

2 Put ice-cream in each bowl. Add drained peaches and kiwi-fruit slices.

3 Pour on some of the raspberry sauce and place a wafer on top.

4 You can add a few chopped nuts or flaked toasted almonds if you wish.

Lollies are water ices. They can be made in **moulds** at home.

Ask your Mum or Dad to help you make some lollies.

What's your favourite flavour of ice-cream? In **California** they even make **garlic**, curry and tomato ice-cream! Do you think you'd like some of that?

Ice-cream

Ice-cream is something
I like to eat,
in summer or winter
it's always a treat.

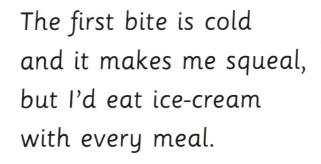

Any flavour
is fine with me,
chocolate, vanilla
or strawberry.

The first bite is cold
and it makes me squeal,
but I'd eat ice-cream
with every meal.

Glossary

Blended When you mix things together they are blended.

California A place on the west coast of the USA, sometimes known as 'The Sunshine State'.

Computer An electronic machine that stores information and can work machinery – in this instance, the running of the mixing plant.

Explorer Someone who travels about in a country and finds out things about it.

Garlic A small plant with a root that has a strong flavour.

Moulds Containers for making something. Jellies and lollies are made in moulds.

Pasteurised The ice-cream mixture is heated to kill any germs.

Sundae Ice-cream served with a topping of fruit, nuts and syrup.

Temperature How hot or cold something is.

Acknowledgements
The author and publisher would like to thank Birds Eye Wall's Limited and the Ice-Cream Federation Limited for their advice.

Notes for parents and teachers

Read the book with children either individually or in groups. Talk about the illustrations as you turn each page. Ask children for their favourite varieties. In the classroom a simple chart could be produced showing favourite ice-creams and questions written to go with it – which ice-cream is liked the most? Which is liked least? Do more boys than girls like one particular kind? Children could also research their families' likes and dislikes. Do older people enjoy different sorts of ice-creams?

What do children know about China? Could they make 'Chinese ice-cream' by mixing fruit juice with water and then freezing it? Children could write about the process and draw 'before' and 'after' pictures to show the change that takes place.

Children might also enjoy making Ice-cream Soda to discover how ice-cream changes when mixed with lemonade.

Suggest that children bring to school ice-cream labels, wrappers and boxes for a display. Talk about the ingredients. These could then be priced and used for simple shopping problems.

Part of the classroom might become an ice-cream café. Children could write menus on ice-cream shaped card.

Stories could be written on such subjects as 'The biggest ice-cream in the world', 'The ice-cream thieves' or 'Meltdown at the ice-cream factory!'

Ask children to collect magazine advertisements for ice-cream. Do they really make children want to try the product? Children may enjoy inventing different ice-creams or lollies. Ask them to list the ingredients and design an advertisement with an eye-catching slogan.

A class letter could be written to Birds Eye Wall's Limited asking for information about ice-cream. The address is Freezeline, Birds Eye Wall's Limited, Station Avenue, Walton-on-Thames, Surrey KT12 1NT.

Children who attempt the recipe will be discovering similarities and differences in the various materials. They will discover how food changes – defrosting frozen raspberries, making sauce from raspberries and icing sugar. Children should also be able to talk about what they have done and to remember the order in which they prepared their sundae. Simple flow charts and diagrams might be produced by older children to show the stages in making the sundae and in the factory production of ice-cream.

The above suggestions will satisfy a number of statements of attainment in National Curriculum guidelines for English, Maths and Science at Key Stage 1.

Books to read

A Packet of Poems Poems about food, selected by
Jill Bennett (OUP 1982).
A Picnic of Poetry Poems about food and drink,
selected by Anne Harvey (Blackie 1988/Puffin 1990).
The Great Ice-Cream Crime by Hazel Townson
(Anderson Young Readers Library, 1981)
Party Food by Clare Beaton (Kingfisher Books 1990)
A–Z: Food by Beverley Mathias and Ruth Thomson
(Franklin Watts 1991)

Index